›› CONTENTS

BOLD I APPROACH

6 TOPICAL BIBLE STUDIES FOR
SMALL GROUPS AND INDIVIDUALS

TONY PAYNE

matthiasmedia

SYDNEY · YOUNGSTOWN

Bold I Approach
Second edition
© Matthias Media 2010

First published 1996

All rights reserved. Except as may be permitted by the Copyright Act, no part of this publication may be reproduced in any form or by any means without prior permission from the publisher.

Matthias Media
(St Matthias Press Ltd ACN 067 558 365)
Email: info@matthiasmedia.com.au
Internet: www.matthiasmedia.com.au
Please visit our website for current postal and telephone contact information.

Matthias Media (USA)
Email: sales@matthiasmedia.com
Internet: www.matthiasmedia.com
Please visit our website for current postal and telephone contact information.

Scripture quotations are from The Holy Bible, English Standard Version® (ESV®), copyright © 2001 by Crossway, a publishing ministry of Good News Publishers. Used by permission. All rights reserved.

ISBN 978 1 921441 82 0

Cover design and typesetting by Matthias Media.
Series concept design by Lankshear Design.

» HOW TO MAKE THE MOST OF THESE STUDIES

1. What is a Topical Bible Study?

Topical Bible Studies are a bit like a guided tour of a famous city. They take you on a tour through the Bible, looking at material related to the topic (in this case, prayer), helping you to know where to start, pointing out things along the way, suggesting avenues for further exploration, and making sure that you know how to get home. Like any good tour, the real purpose is to allow you to go exploring for yourself—to dive in, have a good look around, and discover for yourself the riches that God's word has in store.

In other words, these studies aim to provide stimulation and input and point you in the right direction, while leaving you to do plenty of the exploration and discovery yourself.

These studies are like a tour of a famous city in another sense—they don't hope to look at everything; just the important things. We can't cover in detail everything the Bible says on a given topic, but we do aim to finish our tour without having missed any significant landmarks.

We hope that these studies will stimulate lots of inter-action— interaction with the Bible, with the things we've written, with your own current thoughts and attitudes, with other people as you discuss them, and with God as you talk to him about it all.

2. The format

The studies contain five main components:

- sections of text that introduce, inform, summarize and challenge
- numbered questions that help you examine the passage and think through its meaning
- sidebars that provide extra bits of background or optional extra study ideas, especially regarding other relevant parts of the Bible
- 'Implications' sections that help you think about what this passage means for you and your life today
- suggestions for thanksgiving and prayer as you close.

3. How to use these studies on your own

- Before you begin, pray that God would open your eyes to what he is saying in the Bible, and give you the spiritual strength to do something about it.
- Work through the study, reading the text, answering the questions about the Bible passage, and exploring the sidebars as you have time.
- Resist the temptation to skip over the 'Implications' and 'Give thanks and pray' sections at the end. It is important that we not only hear and understand God's word, but respond to it. These closing sections help us do that.
- Take what opportunities you can to talk to others about what you've learnt.

4. How to use these studies in a small group

- Much of the above applies to group study as well. The studies are suitable for structured Bible study or cell groups, as well as for more informal pairs and triplets. Get together with a friend or friends and work through them at your own pace; use them as the basis for regular Bible study with your spouse. You don't need the formal structure of a 'group' to gain maximum benefit.

- For small groups, it is very useful if group members can work through the study themselves before the group meets. The group discussion can take place comfortably in an hour (depending on how sidetracked you get!) if all the members have done some work in advance.

- The role of the group leader is to direct the course of the discussion and to try to draw the threads together at the end. If you are a group leader, the material in the appendix 'Tips for group leaders' (at the back of this book) is designed to help you think through how to use these studies in a group setting.

- We haven't included an 'answer guide' to the questions in the studies. This is a deliberate move. We want to give you a guided tour of the Bible, not a lecture. There is more than enough in the text we have written and the questions we have asked to point you in what we think is the right direction. The rest is up to you.

5. Bible translation

Previous editions of this Topical Bible Study have assumed that most readers would be using the New International Version of the Bible. However, since the release of the English Standard Version in 2001, many have switched to the ESV for study purposes. So with this new edition of *Bold I Approach*, we have decided to quote from and refer to the ESV text, which we recommend.

GOD AND US

MOST PEOPLE ON THE PLANET pray at least sometime in their lives, usually without giving it much thought, or considering it difficult. Children pray, often with disarming simplicity and ease. When difficulty or danger threatens, the immediate response of many is to pray. At one level, it seems to be the most natural and spontaneous thing in the world.

Yet for Christians, prayer can often seem anything like the easiest thing in the world. We know we ought to pray. We feel, almost instinctively, that prayer should be at the centre of our lives. Yet few areas of our Christian walk cause such a sense of failure and guilt. Few things are so agonizingly difficult as consistent prayer. Few things make us *feel* less like a Christian as when we have gone long periods without praying.

Few things too, it must be said, are the cause of such misunderstanding. While prayer is an almost universal human activity, what is meant by 'prayer' is far from universal. Even among Christians, misleading views and practices of prayer are widespread. And because prayer is a problem area for many of us, we are always ready to listen to anyone offering a new perspective, a missing dimension, or a fail-safe technique.

This set of studies will provide no new secret or technique for solving the 'prayer problem'. There are many such books on the market, their very number indicating that the 'problem' remains unsolved, or at least that the techniques do not work.

Instead, we will follow what should always be our first reflex—to turn to God and listen to him, as he speaks to us in the Bible. We will hear what he has to say about himself, and about us, and about how we can talk to him.

That will be the focus of these studies. We will put our own questions and struggles aside (at least to begin with) to see what God has to say about prayer: what it is, why we should do it, how we should do it, and so on. Having done so, we can come back to our questions and problems, finding perhaps that many of them have been solved by what we have learnt.

The God we pray to

It hardly needs to be said that prayer is an interaction between us and God. It takes place between two parties who have some sort of relationship, and if we are going to understand the first thing about prayer, we must first discover what this relationship is like. More importantly, we must first discover what God is like.

When the Buddhist spins his prayer wheel or the Hindu sits in mystic silence, both are reflecting the nature of the 'god' to whom they are praying. Prayer takes its shape from the deity to whom we pray. Prayer is only possible if the 'god' is willing to accept our prayers; prayer will only be effective if the 'god' is willing and able to answer our prayers.

What sort of God do you pray to? Let us pause and think further about this.

1. How do you think of God as you pray to him? Do you visualize anything? Do you imagine him listening to you?

2. Can you think of any good reason why God should listen or respond to your prayers?

3. What would prayer be like if God was:

   • a life force or energy?

   • a fierce moral policeman?

Throughout the Scriptures, the Bible writers are quite insistent that the true and living God is very different from the idols and pagan gods of the nations.

What sort of God is he? What is it about him that makes prayer possible? And what sort of prayer will he demand or accept?

4. Read Psalm 104:24-30. What is God's basic relationship to the created world?

5. Skim through the following verses. How far does God's power and control extend in the world? What is he able to do?

- Jeremiah 32:17, 26-27

- Proverbs 21:1

- Matthew 10:29

- Acts 2:22-24

- Romans 8:28-30

6. What characteristics of God suggest that he might be willing to listen to our prayers?

- Mark 1:40-41

- Psalm 145:10-21

7. What characteristics of God suggest that we might have some difficulty approaching him in prayer?

- Leviticus 11:44-45

- Psalm 11:4-7

- Psalm 130:1-3

- 1 John 1:5

- 1 Timothy 6:15-16

How to approach an unapproachable God

FROM WHAT WE HAVE LOOKED AT SO FAR, prayer seems both an exciting possibility and a practical impossibility! God is the all-powerful creator and ruler of the world, who delights to show kindness to all who call upon him. And yet he is the blindingly holy, righteous God, whose eyes are too pure to look on evil, and who does not leave the guilty unpunished.

How can sinful and imperfect people like us have any relationship with a God such as this? How can we approach the one who dwells in unapproachable light? And if we cannot approach him with any confidence, how can we hope to speak with him, to make requests and expect him to answer? *How can sinners pray to a holy God?*

The answer to this question is found in the unfolding story of the Bible. It begins with the account of how God created mankind, along with the world and everything in it. It tells of how mankind rebelled against God and was ejected from his holy presence, and how a powerful angel with a flaming sword was stationed at the entrance to the garden of Eden to make any return impossible.

In many ways, the angel with the flaming sword is a symbol of the problem all mankind faces. The way to God is blocked, and we have no way through. As the story of the Bible unfolds, God himself sets about remedying the situation. He takes the initiative to re-establish a relationship with his rebel creation.

It is very important that we understand how this new relationship with God comes about, what it's like, and where it's heading. If we can grasp these simple but crucial things, we will be well on the way to understanding prayer.

Romans 8 is a great place to start looking at these things; it is an awesome chapter. Sadly, we cannot mine all its riches in this study. For our purposes, let us see what it says about the new relationship God establishes with mankind.

Read Romans 8:1-17.

In this passage, two ways of life are contrasted: what we once were, and what we now are.

8. What were we once captive to?

9. What used to be our attitude to God?

10. What is our new relationship with God like? (See especially vv. 1, 6, 10, 15-16.)

11. What role does Christ have in establishing this new relationship? (See especially vv. 1-3.)

12. Looking mainly at verses 9-16, what role does the Spirit have:

- in making us one with Christ?

- in our relationship with the Father?

- in our daily lives?

Read Romans 8:12-25.
13. What belongs to the Christian now, and what is yet to come?

14. What is the nature of the Christian life now, from these verses?

15. Try to write a brief summary of what it means to be a Christian from all that you have studied in Romans 8.

Bold I approach

WHEN WE LOOK AT GOD—AT HOW high and holy he is, and how low and sinful we are—the possibility of successful prayer seems remote indeed. And yet, because of the saving work of Jesus, we are raised up from our low position and granted free access to God the Father Almighty. As Charles Wesley so beautifully put it:

> No condemnation now I dread;
> Jesus, and all in him, is mine!
> Alive in him, my living head,
> and clothed in righteousness divine,
> bold I approach the eternal throne
> and claim the crown
> through Christ my own.[1]

If we can grasp the truth of this, and let it penetrate our minds, then we are already well on the way to understanding prayer. For the new relationship Christians have with the Father, through the Son, in the Spirit, is the beginning and end of true prayer.

Prayer is not an addendum to the Christian life. It is not in a category of its own. It is at the very heart of who we are as Christians, and how we relate to our heavenly Father.

As we shall see in our next study, what it means to be Christian, and what it means to pray, are very nearly the same thing.

» Implications

- In this study, we have looked at how we can have an intimate relationship with God. What other ways do people suggest we can get close to God or relate to him? What do you think of these?

- Given what we have learnt about God, what would you expect praying to him to be like?

- What does your own prayer life reveal about what you really think of God?

- We have thought about how God's character makes prayer possible. Is there anything about God that *demands* prayer; that makes it a necessity?

» Give thanks and pray

- It is only because of Jesus that we can have an intimate relationship with our most Holy God. Thank God for sending Jesus to be our mediator.
- Ask God to open your hearts and minds to his word in the coming weeks as you look at what the Bible says about prayer.
- Pray for each other, that as a result of reading God's word you will respond with heartfelt prayer, enjoying the gift of a personal relationship with our creator.

Endnote
1. Charles Wesley, 'And Can it be that I Should Gain?', 1738.

THE ESSENCE OF PRAYER

GIVEN ALL THAT WE SAW IN OUR first study about the character and power of God, and the new relationship we have with him in Christ, where does prayer fit in? What is prayer exactly? What is it really about?

First, let's recap.

In the majestic verses of Romans 8, a stunning picture of the Christian life is laid out before us. We once were slaves to sin and death and fear, hostile to God and unable to please him. Now we are free sons of the Father and co-heirs of his kingdom with Christ. Through being united with Christ the Son, who died to free us, we now live a new life in which God himself dwells within us by his Spirit.

This new life is ours in hope. Although our relationship with God the Father is assured and we have his Spirit living within us, the final redemption of our bodies is still to come. We live between the times, with one foot in each world.

This is the Christian life, according to Romans 8: a new and ongoing relationship with God the Father through the Son in the Spirit, as we await the glory of the new age.

What has this to do with prayer? The answer is: everything. Prayer only takes place because of this new relationship with the Father through the Son by the Spirit. In fact, prayer is simply this relationship in action. *In essence, prayer is talking to the Father, through the Son, in the Spirit, as we wait for glory.*

Talking...

Prayer in the Bible is always simply and unashamedly *speech*, from us to God. When the disciples ask Jesus to teach them how to pray, he replies: "When you

Praying is saying

Prayer consists of words spoken by us to God. This may be stating the obvious, but sometimes the obvious needs to be stated, especially in light of the different views people have of prayer these days. In other religions, and even according to some Christians, prayer can be any of the following:

- an attitude
- a set of pious thoughts
- wordless ecstasy
- contemplation
- listening
- an action (as in doing something 'as a prayer').

But God is not a force such that we relate to him by feeling him. He is not an idea, such that we relate to him by thinking about him. He is a person, and so we relate to him by listening and speaking. He speaks to us (through the Scriptures); we speak to him in response.

pray, *say*: 'Father, hallowed be your name…'" (Luke 11:2). **Praying is saying.** It is talking to the Father.

It should not surprise us that prayer to the biblical God is speech, since he is a personal God, and speech is how people relate to one another. God for his part has spoken to us at many times and in various ways through the prophets, and in these last days by his Son (Heb 1:1-2). We are given the unspeakable privilege of speaking in return, of pouring out our souls before this God—asking, thanking, crying out, confessing, interceding, and so on (more on this later).

...to the Father, through the Son, in the Spirit...

In particular, prayer in the Bible is talking to God the *Father*. In the garden of Gethsemane, at the time of his greatest distress, Jesus prayed: "Abba, Father, all things are possible for you. Remove this cup from me. Yet not what I will, but what you will" (Mark 14:36). This direct and intimate cry to the Father is ours as well. Now that we are God's children with God's Spirit in our hearts, we too cry out "Abba! Father!" (Rom 8:15; or Gal 4:6).

Let us investigate more of what it means to talk to God as Father, as well as how we do this through the Son, in the Spirit.

1. Read Galatians 4:4-7. How does Jesus' Father become *our* Father? How do we become God's children?

2. Read Matthew 6:25-34 and 7:7-11.

   - How is God a Father to us?

- What do you think this will mean for prayer?

3. From the following references, what is Jesus doing for us now?
   - Romans 8:34

   - Hebrews 7:25

   - 1 John 2:1-2

4. How do we have access to God the Father?
   - Ephesians 2:18

   - Hebrews 4:14-16

   - Hebrews 10:19-23

5. Read Romans 8:26-27. What does the Spirit do in relation to our prayers?

6. Read Ephesians 2:18 and 6:18. Given these verses, and those above, what do you think 'praying in the Spirit' means?

JUST AS OUR RELATIONSHIP WITH the Father can only be through the Son, so also prayer can only take place through the Son. Through his cleansing sacrifice we are granted access to God's throne, sinners though we are. And when we kneel before God to make our requests, we see the same Son at the Father's side, pleading our cause.

The Spirit likewise is essential for Christian prayer, just as he is essential to the Christian life. God's Spirit is the bond that unites us with Christ. He is the Spirit of the Father and Son living within us, leading us to live the Father's way and guaranteeing our inheritance. In other words, just as we have an intercessor in heaven, who gives us access to the Father, so also we have an intercessor *within* (Rom 8:26-28). Because of our weakness and the struggles of living in a sinful world, our prayers are plagued by ignorance and imperfection. Yet God's own Spirit helps us. In a way that is too deep for words, he makes up for our weakness and ignorance by interceding to the Father on our behalf.

...as we wait for glory

This speaking to the Father through the Son in the Spirit doesn't occur in a vacuum. It takes place in a particular context or situation. It happens as we live with the tension of being members of God's family and yet residents of a fallen world. As we speak to God our Father, we do not do so in the comfort and rest of eternal bliss. We speak to him in weakness and suffering as we battle our own continued sinfulness, the temp-

tations and hostility of the world, and the animosity of the devil.

This is why prayer is often a struggle. When Paul mentioned to the Colossians that Epaphras was working hard for them "struggling on [their] behalf in his prayers" (Col 4:12), we can understand what he meant. Prayer can often be a great struggle, both in doing it, and in knowing what to pray—which is why God grants us his Spirit to help and intercede for us (as we saw in Romans 8).

This is also perhaps the reason that God *commands* us to pray. Given all that we have seen so far, such a command almost seems unnecessary. Given who God is, and what he has done for us, how could we *not* pray? Given the staggering privilege of access to a gracious heavenly Father for whom nothing is impossible, how could we be slow to ask him for things? And given also that he graciously promises to hear us, and to grant us every good thing, how could we fail to go to him at every available opportunity?

And yet time and again in the Scriptures, we see God commanding us to pray. "Continue steadfastly in prayer, being watchful in it with thanksgiving", Paul warns the Colossians (Col 4:2). He has similar words for the Ephesians: "[Pray] at all times in the Spirit, with all prayer and supplication. To that end keep alert with all perseverance, making supplication for all the saints" (Eph 6:18).

In our weakness and continued sinfulness, it seems we need more than a promise and a privilege. We need the call of God's command as well, to drive us to our knees and speak to him.

There is much more to be said about the character, content and purpose of prayer. We will return to it in our next study.

Conclusion

The Christian life is about a new father-child relationship. It is about a child who was once not a part of the family, but a sworn enemy of the father and all that he stood for. The father took great pains to win this hostile and wayward child and adopt him into the family, making him an heir of all he possessed, and giving him free and intimate access to himself.

Every Christian is that child. And the father is no ordinary father, but *the* Father—the Lord of the universe, the one from whom all fatherhood derives its name.

Prayer is the conversation between us, as adopted children, and God, as our Father, as we await that time when we will see our Father face to face. Prayer is simply our relationship with God in action, or rather in speech. It is not something extra or additional or optional.

This is why we have taken some lengths in this study to see that prayer has the same essence or basic shape as the Christian life. It is about relating to the Father on the basis of what his Son, Jesus Christ, has achieved, and by the work of his Spirit in our hearts.

It is a simple point, but one that we must establish first of all, to clear up misunderstandings and to provide a solid basis for what is to follow. For there is still much to learn about prayer—about how to do it, why we do it, and why we don't do it.

» Implications

(Choose one or more of the following to think about further or to discuss in your group.)

- How has this study changed your view of prayer?

- In what ways is the Christian life hard work?

- In what ways is prayer hard work? What particular struggles do you have in prayer?

- What is the connection between the good works we do and our relationship with God? Is this any different with prayer?

- "Prayer is how I build my relationship with God. When I pray, I get close to him, and when he answers my prayers I know that he loves me." What is potentially wrong with this statement?

- Read the Lord's Prayer in Matthew 6:9-13. How does it relate to what we have looked at in this study about prayer?

›› Give thanks and pray

- Thank God that because of Jesus and the gift of the Holy Spirit, we can come to him freely, as our Father.
- Practice talking to God, as a perfect Father, without being ashamed or trying to script your prayer beforehand.
- Ask God for help as you continue to struggle with prayer, that you may be consistent and persistent in overcoming the temptation to be lazy in prayer.

» STUDY 3

WHAT USE IS TALK?

WHAT USE IS TALKING TO GOD? This may seem a strange question to ask, especially after all that we have so far discovered about God and our new relationship with him. Do we need any further reasons for prayer apart from the fact that it is possible? If the God of the universe has invited us to talk with him, it seems almost blasphemous to respond by saying, "Yes, but what for?"

All the same, it is a question that very naturally springs to our minds. Prayer can sometimes seem quite pointless to us. If God is the sovereign ruler of the world, what can we ask him that he doesn't already know, or that he hasn't already given us?

There is a part of us that sees prayer as almost a waste of time. We are keen to get on with being Christian, reading the Bible, sharing the gospel, doing works of service, and getting involved in church activities—but prayer? It seems relatively useless compared with actually *doing* something for someone.

What we are really asking is: Does prayer have a purpose? What is its function in our Christian lives? What part does it play? What is the point of praying?

Although these are, in one sense, strange questions to ask, in answering them we will learn some important lessons about the vital part prayer plays in our ongoing relationship with God. According to the Scriptures, talking to God performs *four crucial functions* in our Christian lives, and we will look at the first three of these in this study. (We will examine the fourth, as well as the difficult question of how our prayers and God's sovereign purposes might fit together, in the next study.)

1. In prayer, we grasp hold of God's blessings

Read Romans 10:10-13; 1 John 1:5-2:2; Luke 11:9-13.

1. How do we take hold of the forgiveness and salvation God offers and make it our own?

2. How do we receive the Holy Spirit?

3. What is the relationship between faith (or trusting God) and prayer?

Grasping hold of God's blessings

The Reformer John Calvin expressed the function of prayer like this:

> ...to know God as the master and bestower of all good things, who invites us to request them of him, and still not go to him and not ask of him—this would be of as little profit as for a man to neglect a treasure, buried and hidden in the earth, after it had been ▶

SINCE GOD IS A PERSON, and our relationship with him is personal, it is natural that the way we relate to him is by talking. For his part, God speaks to us and makes certain promises: to forgive those who repent and put their trust in him because of the blood of Christ. For our part, we accept his gracious offer by confessing our sin, begging his forgiveness, and asking for the promised Holy Spirit. By simply talking to God, we **grasp hold** of the blessings that he offers and make them our own.

The blessings of the gospel are not bestowed on us automatically, like a zap from heaven, without any participation or action by us. We receive God's blessings by asking for them, not only at the beginning of our Christian lives but throughout. The whole Christian life is one of

constant repentance, of turning back to the Holy One and away from our sins. Each day of the Christian life is a new day, in which we ask God to forgive us our sins, as we forgive those who sin against us. God does not want us to sin, but knowing that we will, he provides for forgiveness through Christ.

2. In prayer, we give thanks for God's blessings

One cannot read the prayers of the New Testament, and especially those of Paul, without being struck by how full they are of thanksgiving. Having called upon the Lord and received all the rich blessings he offers, Paul never ceases to give thanks to the Father for all that he has received.

This is part of the basic shape of New Testament Christianity. Since God's salvation and all his blessings come to us through his free and undeserved mercy, the immediate and ongoing response of the Christian is thanksgiving. What else would it be? If we earned God's forgiveness, our response might be self-congratulation. But since it all comes by grace, our impulse is to congratulate God, to pour out our thanks to him.

This is true not only of our salvation, but also of all the good things that we receive from God's hand.

pointed out to him... It is, therefore, by the benefit of prayer that we reach those riches which are laid up for us with the Heavenly Father... We dig up by prayer the treasures that were pointed out by the Lord's gospel, and which our faith has gazed upon.[1]

Constant repentance

Again, Calvin puts it well:

The beginning, and even the preparation, of proper prayer is the plea for pardon with a humble and sincere confession of guilt. Nor should anyone, however holy he may be, hope that he will obtain anything from God until he is freely reconciled to him; nor can God chance to be favourable to any but those whom he has pardoned.[2]

4. Read Psalm 107. List some of the many different things the psalmist thanks God for.

5. Is there anything too small or large to thank God for?

6. Look at the thanksgiving prayers Paul speaks about in the following passages. In each of them, what does he thank God for?

- Ephesians 1:15-16

- Philippians 1:3-6

- Colossians 1:3-8

7. When Paul thanks God for people's faith, or for their hope or love, what does this tell us about the source of our faith, hope and love?

3. In prayer, we grow and persevere

IN PRAYER, WE GRASP HOLD OF THE blessings God offers in the gospel; in prayer, we pour out our thanks to him for all that he has done in winning us to himself. But it does not stop there.

As we turn back to the three passages we just looked at, we will see that the Apostle Paul is never content simply to thank God for where his people have come to. He always wants to go further.

8. Look again at the passages in question 6. What does Paul go on to pray for? How does it relate to the thanksgiving he has just made?

- Ephesians 1:17-19 (also compare Ephesians 3:14-19)

- Philippians 1:9-11

- Colossians 1:9-12

IN STUDY 2, WE SAW HOW THE Christian life is lived 'between the times'. We live in a state of tension, being heirs of God's kingdom and members of the age to come, and yet still living here in a sinful, fallen world with all its suffering and evil. This has an important effect on prayer.

9. What do the following passages reveal about:

- the situation or circumstances in which prayer takes place?
- the purpose of prayer in that situation?

Passage	Situation	Purpose
Philippians 4:4-7		
Ephesians 6:10-20		
Romans 8:22-28		
Matthew 6:9-13		

WE HAVE UNCOVERED ONE OF THE most important functions of prayer in our lives as Christians. In the context of our weakness and struggle to persevere, prayer is our ongoing contact with home base. It is God's appointed means for our perseverance and growth. As Paul puts it in 1 Corinthians 3:6-7, it is God who makes things grow—and so it is to God that we go in prayer to ask for grace in the time of need, to ask for growth in our knowledge and faith and love, and to ask that he keep us firm to the end in Christ Jesus.

In other words, prayer has the same 'forward lean' to it as the Christian life. As we saw in study 2, prayer is talking to the Father, through the Son, in the Spirit, *as we wait for glory*. We strain forward, waiting for the return of Christ. As we struggle to persevere and grow amongst all the pressures, difficulties and distractions of life in this world, prayer is part of the way in which we continue to fix our eyes on what is to come. Prayer is not only how we ask God to help us persevere, but is one of the key ways *by which we persevere*. As we devote ourselves to prayer, to talking regularly with our Father, we keep our minds on the job. We **'stay focused'**, as modern athletes say.

To cease from prayer is like a watchman falling asleep, or like an army control not bothering to maintain radio contact with headquarters. In the end, it leads to disaster.

» Implications

- How does what we have learnt about prayer in this study affect:

  - the way we pray?

  - what we pray for?

- If you are dissatisfied with your own Christian life, what should you do about it?

- Do you ever worry that you might not make the distance as a Christian? What should you do?

Staying focused

It is striking how often in the New Testament prayer is talked about in connection with watching and being on the alert:

"Watch and pray that you may not enter into temptation. The spirit indeed is willing, but the flesh is weak." (Matt 26:41)

"Stay awake at all times, praying that you may have strength to escape all these things that are going to take place, and to stand before the Son of Man." (Luke 21:36)

The end of all things is at hand; therefore be self-controlled and sober-minded for the sake of your prayers. (1 Pet 4:7)

[Pray] at all times in the Spirit, with all prayer and supplication. To that end keep alert with all perseverance, making supplication for all the saints. (Eph 6:18)

Continue steadfastly in prayer, being watchful in it with thanksgiving. (Col 4:2)

- "You do not have, because you do not ask", says the Apostle James (Jas 4:2). Does this describe your prayer life? What can you do about it?

» Give thanks and pray

- Thank God for the blessings he has richly bestowed on you.
- Ask God for growth in knowledge, faith and love.
- Ask God to keep you and the other members of your group firm in Christ to the end.
- If you have neglected to pray in the past, take some time now to repent and ask God for forgiveness—and for his help in changing your ways and beginning to pray regularly.

Endnotes

1. John Calvin, 'Prayer, which is the chief exercise of faith, and by which we daily receive God's benefits', in Kirsten Birkett, *The Essence of the Reformation*, Matthias Media, Sydney, 2009, pp. 168-169.
2. ibid., pp. 180-181.

GOD'S FELLOW WORKERS

IN THIS STUDY, WE PICK UP FROM where we left off last time. We have already looked at three of the four crucial functions of prayer in our Christian lives:

1. In prayer, we grasp hold of God's blessings.
2. In prayer, we give thanks for God's blessings.
3. In prayer, we grow and persevere.

Now to the fourth.

4. In prayer, we are God's fellow workers

Just as prayer is how we grow and persevere, so it is the way we help others grow and persevere. In prayer, we become God's fellow workers, participating with him in his grand plan to save his people and bring them into his eternal kingdom.

1. Read 1 Corinthians 3:5-9. What is the relationship between the work we do and the work God does in the gospel?

2. How would prayer fit into this?

3. Read Acts 6:2-4. What two things make up the basic work of the apostles, from which they must not be distracted?

4. Read Philippians 1:19 and Colossians 4:2-4.

   • What role does prayer have in relation to proclaiming the Word?

   • What role does prayer have in Paul's partnership with the Philippians and the Colossians?

5. Read Colossians 4:12. In what ways is Epaphras an example of the type of prayerfulness Paul is urging upon the Colossians earlier in the chapter?

God's work and ours

IN THIS STUDY AND THE PREVIOUS one, we have seen that prayer—far from being useless or unnecessary—performs all kinds of important functions in the Christian life. It is the way God has appointed for us to relate to him, to grab hold of the blessings that he offers, to thank him for them, to grow and persevere in them, and to *work with him* in bringing others to glory as well.

It is God's choice to do it this way, not ours. He has created us the way we are, as creatures in his image who are capable of relating to each other and to him. Just as language is the way we relate to each other as persons, so it is to be the way we relate to our Creator.

We may still ask: But why does God do it this way? Why doesn't he simply do it all himself? Why does he include our prayers in the way he does things? Surely he doesn't need us to ask for something before he does it?

6. Read Philippians 2:12-13. What is the relationship between God's sovereign work and our work in salvation?

7. How does this help us understand prayer?

8. Read Job 42:7-9.

- Does God respond to Job's prayer?

- How does Job's prayer fit into God's plans?

ALTHOUGH THE COMBINATION OF God's sovereignty and human action will always be somewhat mysterious to us, this much is clear: God uses our prayers as part of his work in the world. God does not *need* us to do anything for him—and that goes for everything we do as Christians, whether teaching, preaching, evangelizing, helping, serving or praying. The amazing thing is that God lovingly includes us in his plans all the same. To the enormous privilege of having access to his presence, he adds the privilege of participating with him in his historic plans for the whole world.

All parents will testify to the importance, and the difficulty, of teaching young children to *ask* for things, rather than to demand them or expect them by right. Learning to ask, and ask nicely, is part of growing up. It is part of recognizing that we will always depend on others for things, and that the way to receive them is not to snatch or demand or sit around and hope, but to ask.

God, in his mercy, teaches and instructs us in the same kind of way. He graciously includes our prayers (and our actions) in his purposes. He remains in control, and will achieve what he wants in the end—yet our prayers, and his answers to them, form part of how he does this.

» Implications

- Think about the privilege of being *God's* fellow worker, of being on *his* team, participating in *his* plans. How might this affect the way you pray and what you pray for?

- Is your concern for others (that they become Christians or that they grow as Christians) reflected in your prayers?

- If you were to write a list of all the different ways you serve and help other people, how high would praying for them rate on your list?

- What are some practical ways in which you could be more active as God's fellow worker in prayer? How could you encourage others to do this too?

» Give thanks and pray

- Spend some time praying for the people who came to your mind as you answered the questions above.
- Thank God for the privilege it is to be part of his great plan and work in this world.
- Ask God for something that is currently on your mind or that you have previously thought too small (or big) to bring to him in prayer.

HOW TO PRAY IN 52 WORDS OR LESS

I REMEMBER THE EVENING WELL, although it was nearly 20 years ago now. A group of us in our youth group had decided to get together for a special 'prayer session'. And it seemed to us that if we could do a few things to 'get in the mood', the whole thing would be much more of a success.

We started by conducting trust exercises we had learned in the school drama group—leading people around blindfolded, having people fall backwards and be caught by others, and so on. Then we all lay down in a circle on our backs with our heads towards the centre, held hands and listened to some inspirational music (I think it was John Michael Talbot). Then, with the music continuing softly underneath, someone read an account of the crucifixion. Finally, we turned the lights right down, sat up and faced the centre of the circle, and stared at the single candle that burned softly there.

We had spent nearly an hour preparing, and now we were ready to pray. There was silence. And then more silence. Everyone was feeling so inspired and 'spiritual' that to actually say anything seemed out of place. It would have broken the mood. The silence dragged on. A few people tried to say a few things, but their heart wasn't in it.

After about 45 minutes we called it quits, some declaring the night a great success, others not so sure.

That evening has always stayed in my memory because it captures the problem most Christians face every day when they think about praying. What should it feel like when I pray? Should I kneel or stand? Should I do some meditation or something similar to get in the mood? Is there any length of time I ought to pray for before it really counts as prayer?

And once I get started, what should I pray for? Do I pray for rain for the farmers, or sunshine for my golf game this afternoon? Is it all right to pray that my kids get into a selective high school, or is that selfish? Should I only pray for 'spiritual' things? Are we wasting God's time when we pray for a parking spot?

We're getting down to the nuts and bolts. Having looked at the larger picture of our relationship with God, at what prayer is and how it fits into that relationship, we now turn to the 'how' of prayer. Where can we turn for some teaching on how to actually go about it?

The obvious place is to the Lord himself, who taught his disciples how to pray. In this study, we will look at Jesus' own how-to guide for prayer, in Matthew 6.

The prayer of the kingdom

When Jesus teaches his disciples how to pray using the Lord's Prayer, he is in the middle of a much longer teaching session—the Sermon on the Mount (as it has come to be called). Having begun to preach the good news of the kingdom of heaven (in Matthew 4), Jesus gathers his disciples at the beginning of Matthew 5 and begins to teach them about this kingdom—about who will enter it, and how they will live and work in it.

In this kingdom, all the Old Testament expectations of blessing are fulfilled (Matt 5:1-17). In this kingdom, righteousness is real—it is a matter of the heart, and not merely external obedience (Matt 5:20-48). In this kingdom, God is a heavenly Father (5:16, 45, 48; 6:1, etc.). He reigns over all, sending sun and rain for the just and unjust alike (5:45), and providing all things for his creation (6:25ff.). He sees all (6:6); he knows all (6:8). He is a generous and good Father, longing to give good gifts to his children (7:7-11).

This is the kingdom that we have entered as Christians, a kingdom of personal relationship with God (as our Father) and of real righteousness. It is a unique kingdom, with a kind of prayer that is different from any other. As Jesus says, "When you pray, do not heap up empty phrases as the Gentiles do, for they think that they will be heard for their many words. Do not be like them, for your Father knows what you need before you ask him" (6:7-8).

What is prayer like in the kingdom of God?

Read Matthew 6:1-8.

1. How is 'kingdom prayer' different from the prayer of the religious hypocrites?

2. What does the person who prays to be seen by others really want? Does he receive it? Who from?

3. How is 'kingdom prayer' different from the prayers of the Gentiles?

4. From verses 7-8, what two mistakes do the Gentiles make about God and prayer?

LIKE EVERYTHING ELSE IN THE kingdom of God, prayer is in great contrast to both the religious ritual of the Pharisees and the ignorance of the Gentiles. As Jesus teases out the differences, a wonderful picture of Christian prayer emerges. There is no complicated ritual or technique, no showy display of religiosity or exaggerated fervour, no babbling on for hours on end to twist God's arm. Instead, there is a simple and bold address to a loving heavenly Father, followed by six equally simple and direct requests.

Read Matthew 6:9–13.

5. How is this prayer an example of the lessons of verses 8-9?

6. Try to summarize what you think each of the six requests is about in your own words.

- hallowed be your name

- your kingdom come

- your will be done

- daily bread

- forgiveness

- temptation/evil

Read Matthew 6:25–34.

7. How are kingdom dwellers to be different from the Gentiles?

8. How do you think this relates to the prayer for "daily bread"?

God's concerns

THE FIRST THREE REQUESTS IN THE Lord's Prayer concern themselves directly with God. This in itself is a challenge to much of our prayer! Prayer in God's kingdom quite naturally starts with God himself, and with his glory. Our Father's concerns are our concerns.

The first of these is that *God's name would be made holy* ("hallowed"). This is a request that the Father would be honoured by all; that no-one would speak or think of him without the fear and reverence that his majestic holiness and power should call forth. It is a prayer that God's person and character would be seen to be holy in the sight of all the world.

This leads naturally to the second request: that *the kingdom should come*. In Matthew's Gospel, Jesus has already been preaching that the kingdom has come near because of his own presence.

With Jesus, God's kingdom does arrive. It enters into history, and we in turn can enter into it. But as we have seen in earlier studies, the kingdom is also still to come. We enjoy its benefits, yet we wait for its fullness. We pray that the curtain will be drawn back, and God's rule will be made plain to everyone.

This in turn leads us to pray for *God's will to be done on earth as in heaven*. We want God's name to be hallowed; we long for that day when every knee will bow and every tongue confess (Phil 2:9-10); yet in the meantime we want to see God's rule (which is his kingdom) advancing on earth. We want men and women to bow their knees now to the Father in repentance and obedience, rather than be forced to at the end of the age. We pray that the way things are in heaven would increasingly become the way they are on earth.

All this is very forward-looking, and fits with what we have already seen about prayer in our earlier studies. Prayer leans towards the future, as does the Christian life in general. It longs and waits for the glory of the coming kingdom. Just as our whole Christian lives are pulled along by the momentous events of the coming kingdom, so our prayers are also to focus on these things.

Our concerns

The fourth request then seems to mark a change in direction. Having prayed for the great concerns of the kingdom, the next request is for a loaf of bread. What do we make of this?

Note that the way the request is framed is a little strange. It is not simply, "Give us the bread we need"; nor is it, "Please supply all our ongoing physical requirements". There is a strong emphasis on the *daily* nature of it. It is a prayer for the bread we need right now—in the next 24 hours—rather than the bread we need during the next 12 months.

This is because the reality of the **coming kingdom** changes everything, including our attitude to food and clothing and our physical needs. And so our request is for *daily* bread, for our immediate needs, not for a car and a boat and a nice big storehouse of bread to do us for the rest of the year.

We can see how this fits into the flow of the Lord's Prayer. We turn to our concerns—what we're going to eat—but they are still kingdom-style concerns. Just as the first three requests looked forward to the coming kingdom, anxiously waiting and praying for it, so the second set of three requests also focuses on the coming kingdom as it affects us now.

The other two requests (for forgiveness and deliverance) also demonstrate this. They also have this future-focus. As the beatitude puts it, only the pure in heart will see God (Matt 5:8); and therefore we need mercy. We need forgiveness of sins. As we look to the coming kingdom, we beg for mercy that we might enter it.

We also beg that our Father would protect us as we

The coming kingdom

When we look further into Matthew 6 the focus on the needs of the moment makes a lot of sense. In light of the importance of the coming kingdom, everything changes. We are not to seek many possessions and store up treasures on earth, for our focus is on the coming kingdom. That is where our hearts should be, and where our treasure should be stored (vv. 19-21). Similarly, we are not to run after food and drink and clothes, for God knows that we need these things and will provide them for us. We must seek above all else God's kingdom and ▶

wait for the coming kingdom in the midst of this present evil age. Will we come through? Is it possible that we might endure; that we might survive the time of testing and the day of evil, and remain God's faithful servants? We want to survive—desperately—and we know only too well our own weakness and frailty. And so we pray for God's leading and deliverance, that he might shelter us from temptation (or 'testing') and might finally deliver us from the evil that pervades our world, personified in the form of the Evil One, Satan.

righteousness, and let the needs of the future be for the future. "Therefore do not be anxious about tomorrow, for tomorrow will be anxious for itself. Sufficient for the day is its own trouble" (v. 34).

Getting down to it

The Lord's Prayer is only 52 words long (in the ESV translation). It is so simple and so direct, and yet so profound in what it teaches us about prayer and about the coming kingdom.

It teaches us that our speech to God, like our whole existence, is shaped and driven by God's kingdom. In entering that kingdom, we have been caught up into God's plans for the whole world. We naturally pray for the glory of his name, the coming of his kingdom, the doing of his will. And as we turn to pray for our own concerns and anxieties, they too are shaped or influenced by the kingdom.

But what of the parking spot? Can we pray for anything we like, or are we only permitted to pray for 'big' things or 'spiritual' things? The Lord's Prayer only goes part of the way towards answering this question. It invites us to pray for the kingdom as it affects both God and us, and we pray this with great confidence because we know that God is bringing in his kingdom. We know that he has promised to give us our daily bread, and to grant us forgiveness, and so we can also pray for these things knowing that God will answer our prayers.

In other words, the Lord's Prayer calls on us to pray for things that God wants us to pray for and has promised to give us. But what of those things which God has not promised? He has not promised, for example, to heal my friend of his sickness, but does that mean I cannot ask him to? The answer is: Of course I can ask God to heal my friend, for God invites us to cast all our anxieties on him (1 Pet 5:7). However, I cannot be sure that it is God's plan to heal my friend at this time. And so I pray for my friend, and leave it with God.

There are some things, then, which we can pray for with great certainty and confidence, because God has promised or commanded them—and if we are to follow the teaching of Jesus, these things should figure heavily in our prayers. There are other matters in which God has not revealed his will to us, but which we are nevertheless free to bring to our loving Father because of the relationship we have with him in Christ, trusting in his goodness and in his eternal wisdom to do what is best.

» Implications

(Choose one or more of the following to think about further or to discuss in your group.)

- Will any particular posture or length of prayer make God more likely to hear us?

- Can you think of some modern examples of the problems Jesus talks about in Matthew 6:1-8?

- When are you in most danger of 'false show' or phoniness in your prayers?

- How has this study changed your view of prayer?

- Does Christian prayer have anything to do with technique? In what ways is Christian prayer different from the prayer of other religions?

- Some Christian traditions say the Lord's Prayer over and over again as a means of gaining God's favour. What do you think Jesus would say about this?

- What is good and what is bad about all-night prayer vigils?

- In study 2, we defined prayer as *talking to the Father, through the Son, in the Spirit, as we wait for glory.* How does this fit with the Lord's Prayer?

- The Lord's Prayer shows us how to pray, rather than giving us the only words we are ever allowed to pray. List out the six petitions of the Lord's Prayer. What things could you pray for under these headings? How might you use the Lord's Prayer as a model for your prayer life?

» Give thanks and pray

- Thank God for Jesus' teaching about kingdom prayer.
- Pray through the Lord's Prayer (in your own words if you like), focusing on what you are actually praying for.
- Praise God for being a God who takes care of our needs, and ask him to help you to stay focused on his kingdom and not the things of this world.
- Pray for some of the things you wrote down under the last question in the 'Implications' section.

PRAYER FROM OUR SIDE

Most years begin something like this for me:

> New Year's Resolution 14: In the interests of domestic harmony, must stop leaving shoes under coffee table.

> New Year's Resolution 15: Get golf handicap down to 10.

> New Year's Resolution 16: In interests of domestic harmony, must reconcile myself to golf handicap remaining at 29.

> New Year's Resolution 17: Must pray more this year.

Like spending more time with the children, or being more involved in evangelism, prayer is something we always feel we could do more of. Ask even the most saintly Christians about their prayer lives, and they will rub their chins and say, "Well, it has its ups and downs. I'm struggling a bit at the moment…"

This is the strange thing about prayer. As we have examined what the Bible teaches about our prayer, the overall picture has been one of great simplicity and directness. Christian prayer is not a complicated technique or elaborate mystical ritual. It is simple speech, directed to our Heavenly Father on the basis of what he has done for us in his Son, through the enabling of his Spirit.

And yet as we actually get down to praying, it is often a struggle. Why is this? If prayer is so simple, why do we often find it so hard?

There are three main reasons—three enemies of prayer—and they will be the focus of this study.

1. What do you find most difficult about prayer?

2. What excuses do you use (or have you heard others use) for not praying?

3. Do you think it is harder to pray in the 21st century than in earlier times? Why/why not?

The enemy within

WHEN IT COMES TO PRAYER, WE ARE our own worst enemies. Although we have a new relationship with God as our Father through his Son, and we have the Spirit of the Father and the Son dwelling in us, we are not perfect—at least not yet. Until that day when Jesus comes in glory, we remain sinners. We continue to flirt with unbelief. We retain some of the twisted thought patterns and habits of our former life. We continue to be tempted, like the Israelites, to return to Egypt.

In other words, prayer is a struggle for the same reason that the Christian life as a whole is a struggle. We live with an inner conflict, as Paul puts it in Galatians 5: "But I say, walk by the Spirit, and you will not gratify the desires of the flesh. For the desires of the flesh are against the Spirit, and the desires of the Spirit are against the flesh, for these are opposed to each other, to keep you from doing the things you want to do" (Gal 5:16-17).

Like the disciples in Gethsemane,

though our Lord has bidden us to watch and pray, and though we know just how important a task this is, we still fall asleep. It is important to realize that this is the nature of things, and it will remain so until the dawn of the next age. We struggle, we strive, we even make progress—but the battle doesn't cease. The imperfect will not disappear until the perfect comes (1 Cor 13:9-10).

This ongoing battle with our own sinfulness is often fought at the level of the things we tell ourselves to avoid praying, the excuses we make. Most of them are pretty woeful, but at 6:45am on a cold morning when we don't feel like praying, these excuses can be powerfully effective. Let's think about some of them.

4. Try to write answers to the following excuses for not praying by thinking back over what we've learnt in previous studies, and by looking up the Bible verses.

- *God is in control. Whether I pray or not won't make any difference. So I won't bother.* (Jas 5:16-18)

What do the following verses say about God's plans and our prayers?

- Exodus 8:28-32

- Philippians 1:19

- *I am too busy to pray.* (Luke 10:38-42; 1 Cor 7:4-5)

- *I am too spiritually dry to pray. I would feel like a phoney.* (Rom 12:12; Luke 18:1-8; Phil 4:6-7)

In Philippians 4:6-7, does the feeling come before or after prayer? Another way of asking this question: Do our feelings diminish our obligation to obey God?

5. What other excuses do you make not to pray? How would you answer them?

6. Read Psalm 66:16-20 and James 4:1-3. In what ways can our sinfulness hinder our prayers?

The enemy without

OUR STRUGGLES WITH PRAYER ARE not only internal. The world around us is also hostile to prayer, in the same way that it is hostile to our Master: "If the world hates you, know that it has hated me before it hated you. If you were of the world, the world would love you as its own; but because you are not of the world, but I chose you out of the world, therefore the world hates you" (John 15:18-19).

In our own age this hostility takes several forms. At one level, the world is deeply *sceptical* about prayer. In a world of hard facts and science, of micro-surgery and antibiotics and relentless technological progress, many regard prayer as the pathetic last resort of the feeble-minded.

As Christians, of course we would object vigorously to this way of thinking, yet we cannot entirely escape its influence. We have all been raised with it. Modern thought is based on the assumption that physical matter is all that exists; that there is nothing and no-one 'upstairs'. Our education system and popular culture drip this assumption into us from an early age. We grow up with a passion for the material and the concrete, for things which are testable and which 'work'. All this tells against prayer. Why pray for healing, after all, when you can take an antibiotic?

This creeping scepticism is particularly strong in the 21st century, but it is certainly nothing new. Let us look at how the psalmist saw it, before considering another form of prayer-attack in James 4.

Read Psalm 14:1-5.

7. What stems from the fool's rejection of God?

8. What does this psalm reveal about the moral state of mankind?

9. How does this compare with modern views? How might this affect prayer, especially prayer for mercy?

Read James 4:1–10.

10. What is wrong with the prayers of the people James is writing to?

11. How is their relationship with the world affecting their prayers? In what sense are they "double-minded"?

12. How can we resist the devil's involvement in all this?

The enemy below

IT IS NOT ONLY IN JAMES THAT WE find prayer and the devil mentioned in the same breath. At different points throughout the Bible, we see Satan assaulting the faith of God's people, and therefore their prayers.

In Ephesians 6, the devil is likened to a manic dart player, hurling flaming missiles at us which can only be quenched by the shield of faith. It is not without reason that Paul goes on to urge us to "[pray] at all times in the Spirit, with all prayer and supplication. To that end keep alert with all perseverance, making supplication for all the saints" (Eph

6:18). In 1 Peter 5, we read similar thoughts: "Humble yourselves, therefore, under the mighty hand of God so that at the proper time he may exalt you, casting all your anxieties on him, because he cares for you. Be soberminded; be watchful. Your adversary the devil prowls around like a roaring lion, seeking someone to devour" (1 Pet 5:6-8).

An awareness of the activities of our 'enemy below' should keep us watchful and alert in prayer. Prayer is the last thing Satan wants us to do, for prayer springs from and reinforces our trust in the Lord. He does all he can to foster our own foolishness, and our compromises with the world, so that our prayers might be infrequent and selfish.

Conclusion

Given the things that are against us, is it any wonder that many Christians find prayer a struggle! In our despair of ever making progress, it is tempting simply to give up trying. We hear stories of the great 'prayer warriors' of the past praying for three hours before breakfast because they were so busy they couldn't afford not to (or some such thing), and our hearts sink. We can manage barely three minutes before breakfast.

Yet we must keep remembering that prayer is no different from the rest of our Christian lives. In fact, prayer is the Christian life in action, or rather in speech, before God. It is our trust in God verbalized, as we pour out before him our struggles, our foolishness, our enemies, our friends, our unbelief, our sin.

The reason that there is hope in the face of all that seems to quench prayer is precisely the same reason that there is any hope at all in the Christian life. It is because of God and his mighty power, which is at work in us who believe. It is only by his grace and the work of the Spirit that we can pray in the first place, having had our eyes opened and been granted access to the Father through Christ. And it is only by God's continued grace, and the continued work of the Spirit, that we can continue to pray.

As we saw in Romans 8, nothing will separate us from the love of Christ. God knows our weakness, and our sin. There is no reason for unrelieved guilt or despair about prayer, any more than there is with regard to the rest of our Christian lives. When we stumble and fall, we beg God's forgiveness. We ask him to pick us up, dust us off and set us walking once again along the road to heaven.

So it is with our Christian walk, and so it is with prayer.

» Implications

- Think back over this study. What things work together to make prayer difficult from our side?

- How do you see your own sinfulness affecting your prayers? Are there things you need to repent of?

- What have you learnt that might help in your own struggles with prayer?

- Thinking back over all the studies, what have you learnt about prayer? Has your view of prayer changed?

- What practical steps do you intend to take in order to "continue steadfastly in prayer"? (See appendix 1 for more practical tips.)

» Give thanks and pray

- Ask our almighty God to deliver you from the temptation not to pray. Ask him to help you struggle on in prayer and ignore the enemy below.
- Thank God that, through Jesus, he has defeated the devil so that we are no longer slaves to sin and can call on our heavenly Father for all our needs.
- Share with each other the things you wrote down under the last question in the 'Implications' section, and pray about them. Also remember to *keep* praying for other members of the group over the coming months, and *asking* them how their struggles with prayer are going.

» LESSONS FROM THE SCHOOL OF PRAYER

[DA CARSON]

Having delved into what the Scriptures teach us about prayer, it is also useful to get some practical tips from other Christians about how to deal with our struggles in prayer. This appendix by Don Carson does just that.[1] It is abridged (by permission) from his excellent book *A Call to Spiritual Reformation*. If you are using these studies in a small group, you might like to use the questions at the end as a basis for group discussion.

THROUGHOUT MY SPIRITUAL pilgrimage, two sources have largely shaped, and continue to shape, my own prayer life: the Scriptures and more mature Christians. The less authoritative of these two has been the advice, wisdom and example of senior saints. I confess I am not a very good student in the school of prayer. Still, devoting a few pages to their advice and values may be worthwhile. Among the lessons more mature Christians have taught me, then, are these.

1. We do not pray because we do not plan to pray

We do not drift into spiritual life; we do not drift into disciplined prayer. We will not grow in prayer unless we plan to pray. That means we must self-consciously set aside time to do nothing but pray.

What we actually do reflects our highest priorities. That means we can proclaim our commitment to prayer until the cows come home, but unless we actually pray, our actions disown our words.

This is the fundamental reason why set times for prayer are important: they ensure that vague desires for prayer are concretized in regular practice. Paul's many references to his "prayers" (e.g. Rom 1:10; Eph 1:16; 1 Thess 1:2) suggest that he set aside specific times for prayer—as apparently Jesus himself did (Luke 5:16). Of course, mere regularity in such matters does not ensure that effective praying takes place: genuine godliness is so easily aped, its place usurped by its barren cousin, formal religion. It is also true that different lifestyles demand different patterns: a shiftworker, for instance, will have to keep changing his or her scheduled prayer times, while a mother of twin two-year-olds will enjoy neither the energy nor the leisure of someone living in less constrained circumstances. But after all the difficulties have been duly recognized, and all the dangers of legalism properly acknowledged, the fact remains that unless we plan to pray we will not pray.

2. Adopt practical ways to impede mental drift

Anyone who has been on the Christian way for a while knows there are times when our private prayers run something like this: "Dear Lord, I thank you for the opportunity of coming into your presence by the merits of Jesus. It is a wonderful blessing to call you Father... I wonder where I left my car keys? [No, no! Back to business.] Heavenly Father, I began by asking that you will watch over my family—not just in the physical sphere, but in the moral and spiritual dimensions of our lives... Boy, last Sunday's sermon was sure bad. I wonder if I'll get that report written on time? [No, no!] Father, give real fruitfulness to that missionary couple we support, whatever their names are... Oh, my! I had almost forgotten I promised to fix my son's bike today..." Or am I the only Christian who has ever had problems with mental drift?

But you can do many things to stamp out daydreaming, to stifle reveries. One of the most useful things is to vocalize your prayers. This does not mean they have to be so loud that they become a distraction to others, or worse, a kind of pious showing off. It simply means you articulate your prayers, moving your lips perhaps; the energy devoted to expressing your thoughts in words and sentences will order and discipline your mind, and help deter meandering.

Another thing you can do is pray over the Scriptures. Christians just setting out on the path of prayer sometimes pray for everything they can think of, glance at their watches, and discover they have been at it for all of three or four minutes. This experience sometimes generates feelings of defeat, discouragement, even despair. A great way to begin to overcome this problem is to pray through various biblical passages.

A slight variation of this plan is to adopt as models several biblical prayers. Read them carefully, think through what they are saying, and pray analogous prayers for yourself, your family, your church, and for many others beyond your immediate circle.

Similarly, praying through the worship sections of the better hymnals can prove immensely edifying and will certainly help you to focus your mind and heart in one direction for a while.

Some pastors pace as they pray. One senior saint I know has long made it his practice to pray through the Lord's Prayer, thinking through the implications of each petition as he goes, and organizing his prayers around those implications.[2] Many others make prayer lists of various sorts, a practice that will be discussed in more detail later.

This may be part of the discipline of what has come to be called 'journalling'. At many periods in the history of the church, spiritually mature and disciplined Christians have kept what might be called spiritual journals. The real value of journalling, I think, is several-fold: (a) It enforces a change of pace, a slowing down. It ensures time for prayer. If you are writing your prayers, you are not daydreaming. (b) It fosters self-examination. It is an old truism that only the examined life is worth living. If you do not take time to examine your own heart, mind and conscience from time to time in the light of God's word, and deal with what you find, you will become encrusted with the barnacles of destructive self-righteousness. (c) It ensures quiet articulation both of your spiritual direction and of your prayers, and this in turn fosters self-examination and therefore growth. Thus, journalling impedes mental drift.

But this is only one of many spiritual disciplines. The danger in this one, as in all of them, is that the person who is formally conforming to such a regime may delude himself or herself into thinking that the discipline is an end in itself, or ensures one of an exalted place in the heavenlies.

Such dangers aside, you can greatly improve your prayer life if you combine these first two principles: set apart time for praying, and then use practical ways to impede mental drift.

3. At various periods in your life, develop, if possible, a prayer-partner relationship

Incidentally, if you are not married, make sure your prayer partner is someone of your own sex. If you are married and choose a prayer partner of the opposite sex, make sure that partner is your spouse. The reason is that real praying is an immensely intimate business— and intimacy in one area frequently leads to intimacy in other areas.

While I was still an undergraduate, in one summer vacation a single pastor took me aside and invited me to pray with him. We met once a week, on Monday nights, for the next three months. Sometimes we prayed for an hour or so, sometimes for much longer. But there is no doubt that he taught me more of the rudiments of prayer than anyone else.

At various periods of my life, other such opportunities have come my way. For the last year or so of my doctoral study, another graduate student and I set aside time one evening a week to pray. Eventually (I was rather slow on this front), I got married. Like most couples, we have found that sustained time for prayer together is not easy to maintain. Not only do we live at a hectic pace, but each stage of life also has its peculiar pressures. When you have two or three pre-school-aged children, for instance, you are up early and exhausted by the evening. Still, we have tried to follow a set pattern. Quite apart from grace at meals, which may extend beyond the expected "thank you" to larger concerns, and quite apart from individual times for prayer and Bible reading, as a family we daily seek God's face. About half the time my wife or I lead the family in prayer; the rest of the time, the children join us in prayer. We have discovered the importance of injecting freshness and innovation into such times, but that is another subject. Before we retire at night, my wife and I invariably pray together, usually quite briefly. But in addition, at various points in our life together we have tried to set aside some time one evening a week to pray. Usually we achieve this for a few weeks, and then something breaks it up for a while. But we have tried to return to it, and we use those times to pray for family, church, students, pressing concerns of various sorts, our children, our life's direction and values, impending ministry, and much more.

If you know how to pray, consider seeking out someone else and teaching him or her how to pray. By teaching I do not mean set lessons so much as personal example communicated in a prayer-partner relationship. Such modelling and partnership will lead to the sorts of questions that will invite further sharing and discipleship. After all, it was because Jesus' disciples observed his prayer life that they sought his instruction in prayer (Luke 11:1).

4. Choose models—but choose them well

Most of us can improve our praying by carefully, thoughtfully listening to others pray. This does not mean we should copy everything we hear. Some people use an informal and chatty style in prayer that reflects their own personality and perhaps the context in which they were converted; others intone their prayers before God with genuine erudition coupled with solemn formality, deploying vocabulary and forms of English considered idiomatic 350 years ago. Neither extreme is an intrinsically good model; both might be good models, but not because of relatively external habits, and certainly not because of merely cultural or personal idiosyncrasy. When we find good models, we will study their content and urgency, but we will not ape their idiom.

Not every good model provides us with exactly the same prescription for good praying, exactly the same balance. All of them pray with great seriousness; all of them use arguments and seek goals that are already portrayed in Scripture. Some of them seem to carry you with them into the very throne room of the Almighty; others are particularly faithful in intercession, despite the most difficult circumstances in life and ministry; still others are noteworthy because of the breadth of their vision. All are characterized by a wonderful mixture of contrition and boldness in prayer.

Once again, my life has been blessed by some influential models. I must begin by mentioning my own parents. I remember how, even when we children were quite young, each morning my mother would withdraw from the hurly-burly of life to read her Bible and pray.

In the years that I was growing up, my father, a Baptist minister, had his study in our home. Every morning we could hear him praying in that study. My father vocalized when he prayed—loudly enough that we knew he was praying, but not loudly enough that we could hear what he was saying. Every day he prayed, usually for about 45 minutes. Perhaps there were times when he failed to do so, but I cannot think of one.

But with great gratitude to God, I testify that my parents were not hypocrites. That is the worst possible heritage to leave with children: high spiritual pretensions and low performance. My parents were the opposite: few pretensions, and disciplined performance. What they prayed for were the important things, the things that congregate around the prayers of Scripture. And sometimes when I look at my own children, I wonder if, should the Lord give us another thirty years, they will remember their father as a man of prayer, or think of him as someone distant who was away from home rather a lot and who wrote a number of obscure books. That quiet reflection often helps me to order my days.

5. Develop a system for your prayer lists

It is difficult to pray faithfully for a large spread of people and concerns without developing prayer lists that help you remember them. These lists come in a variety of forms. Many denominations and mission agencies and even some large local churches publish their own prayer lists. These can be a considerable help to those with large interest in the particular organization; otherwise, they may seem a trifle remote. Despite its remoteness, there is one prayer list that offers a tremendous compensating advantage. The list to which I am referring is the publication *Operation World* which, over the course of a year, takes you around the world to country after country and region after region, and provides you with succinct, intelligent information to assist you in your prayers.[3] Its value lies in its ability to enlarge your horizons, to expand your interest in the world church and the world's needs.

Many Christians who give themselves to prayer, however, find that, in addition to such published information, it is wise and fruitful to prepare their own lists. These come in many forms. Some are really a subset of journalling, briefly described earlier in this chapter. One approach to journalling involves writing down prayer requests on the left-hand side of a notebook, along with a date and relevant Scriptures, and answers on the right-hand side. This approach has the advantage of encouraging thoughtful, specific requests. General intercession, as important as it may be, cannot so easily be linked to specific answers.

Although I have sometimes adopted this and other forms for my prayer lists, the prayer-list pattern I have followed in recent years I adapted from J Herbert Kane, a veteran missionary to China (1935-1950) and then a productive teacher of world mission. Apart from any printed guides I may use, I keep a manila folder in my study, where I pray, and usually I take it with me when I am travelling. The first sheet in that folder is a list of people for whom I ought to pray regularly: they are bound up with me, with who I am. My wife heads the list, followed by my children and a number of relatives, followed in turn by a number of close friends in various parts of the world. The two institutional names on that sheet are the local church of which we are a part, and the seminary where I now teach.

The second sheet in my folder lists short-range and intermediate-range concerns that will not remain there indefinitely. They include forthcoming responsibilities in ministry and various crises or opportunities that I have heard about, often among Christians I scarcely know. Either they are the sort of thing that will soon pass into history, or they concern people or situations too remote for me to remember indefinitely.

The next item in my manila folder is the list of my advisees—the students for whom I am particularly responsible. This list includes some notes on their background, academic program, families, personal concerns and the like, and of course this list changes from year to year.

The rest of the folder is filled with letters—prayer letters, personal letters, occasionally independent notes with someone's name at the top. These are filed in alphabetical order. When a new letter comes in, I highlight any matters in it that ought to be the subject of prayer, and then file it in the appropriate place in the folder. The letter it replaces is pulled out at the same time, with the result that the prayer folder is always up to date. I try to set aside time to intercede with God on behalf of the people and situations represented by these letters, taking the one on the top, then the next one, and the next one, and so forth, putting the top ones, as I finish with them, on the bottom of the pile. Thus, although the list is alphabetized, on any day a different letter of the alphabet may confront me. As I write these lines, I see that names beginning with 'F' are next in the folder.

I am not suggesting that this is the best system. It suits me, and I am happy with it. I need to use it more, not enlarge it more. But the system is flexible, always up-to-date, and expandable; above all, it helps me pray. I tell my students that if they want me to pray for them regularly after they graduate, they need to write regular letters to me. Otherwise I shall certainly forget most of them.

Whatever the system, use prayer lists. All of us would be wiser if we would resolve never to put people down, except on our prayer lists.

6. Mingle praise, confession, and intercession; but when you intercede, try to tie as many requests as possible to Scripture

Both theoretical and practical considerations underlie this advice.

The theoretical considerations can

best be set out by mentally conjuring up two extremes. The first judges it inappropriate to ask God for things. Surely he is sovereign: he does not need our counsel. If he is the one "who works all things according to the counsel of his will" (Eph 1:11), surely it is a bit cheeky to badger him for things. He does not change the course of the universe because some finite, ignorant and sinful human being asks him to. The appropriate response to him, surely, is worship. We should worship him for what he is and does. Because we so frequently skirt his ways, we should be ready to confess our sin. But to bring him our petitions is surely to misrepresent where true piety lies. Godliness rests in submission to the Almighty's will, not in intercession that seeks to change that will. Petitionary prayer can therefore be dismissed as at best an impertinence, at worst a desperate insult to the sovereign and holy God. Besides, if God is really sovereign, he is going to do whatever he wants to do, whether or not he is asked to do it. Of course, if a Christian adopts this line, he or she is thinking in much the same way as a Muslim: the right approach to God binds you to a kind of theological determinism, not to say fatalism.

The second extreme begins with the slogan 'Prayer changes things'. Petitionary prayer is everything. This means that if people die and go to hell, it is because you or I or someone has neglected to pray. Does not Scripture say, "You do not have, because you do not ask" (Jas 4:2)? Worship and confession must of course be allotted an appropriate part, but they can reduce to mere self-gratification: it can be fun to worship, a relief to confess your sins. Real work for God, however, demands that we wrestle with God, and cry, with Jacob, "I will not let you go unless you bless me" (Gen 32:26). Not to intercede is to flee from your responsibilities as a Christian. Far from being an insult to God, petitionary prayer honours him because he is a God who likes to give his blessings in response to the intercession of his people. In fact, if you agonize in your prayers, fast much, plead the name of Jesus, and spend untold hours at this business of intercession, you cannot help but call down from heaven a vast array of blessings. Of course, if a Christian adopts this line, he or she is in danger of treating prayer much like magic: the right incantations produce the desired effect.

On the face of it, neither of these extremes captures the balance of biblical prayers, and both of them are reductionistic in their treatment of God. We must remember that the Bible simultaneously pictures God as utterly sovereign, and as a prayer-hearing and prayer-answering God. Unless we perceive this, and learn how to act on these simultaneous truths, not only will our views of God be distorted, but our praying is likely to wobble back and forth between a resigned fatalism that asks for nothing and a badgering desperation that exhibits little real trust.

Of the various models that usefully capture both of these poles, the model of a personal relationship with a father is as helpful as any. If a boy asks his father for several things, all within the father's power to give, the father may give him one of them right away, delay giving him another, decline to give him a third, set up a condition for a fourth. The child is not assured of receiving something because he has used the right incantation: that would be magic. The father may decline to give something because he knows it is not in the child's best interests. He may delay giving something else because he knows that so many requests from his young son are temporary and whimsical. He may also withhold something that he knows the child needs until the child asks for it in an appropriate way. But above all, the wise father is more interested in a relationship with his son than in merely giving him things. Giving him things constitutes part of that relationship but certainly not all of it. The father and son may enjoy simply going out for walks together. Often the son will talk with his father not to obtain something, or even to find out something, but simply because he likes to be with him.

None of these analogies is perfect, of course. But it is exceedingly important to remember that prayer is not magic and that God is personal as well as sovereign. There is more to praying than asking, but any sustained prayer to the God of the Bible will certainly include asking. And because we slide so easily into sinful self-centredness, we must approach this holy God with contrition and confession of our sins. On other occasions we will focus on his love and forbearance, on the sheer splendour of his being, and approach him with joy and exuberant praise. The rich mixture of approaches to God mirrored in Scripture must be taken over into our own lives. This rich mixture is, finally, nothing more than a reflection of the many different components of the kind of relationship we ought to have with the God of the Bible.

In addition to these 'theoretical' considerations (as I have called them), there are some intensely practical questions. If the one to whom we pray is the sort of God I have just portrayed, then when we ask him for things, when we intercede with him, we must not think either in fatalistic terms or in terms of magic. Rather, we must think in personal and relational categories. We ask our heavenly Father for things because he has determined that many blessings will come to us only through prayer. Prayer is his ordained means of conveying his blessings to his people. That means we must pray according to his will, in line with his values, in conformity with his own character and purposes, claiming his own promises. Practically speaking, *how do we do that?*

Where shall we learn the will of God, the values of God, the character and purposes of God, the promises of God? We shall learn such things in the Scriptures he has graciously given us. But that means that when we pray, when we ask God for things, we must try to tie as many requests as possible to Scripture. That is an immensely *practical* step.

7. If you are in any form of spiritual leadership, work at your public prayers

It does not matter whether the form of spiritual leadership you exercise is the teaching of a Sunday school class, pastoral ministry, small group evangelism, or anything else: if at any point you pray in public as a leader, then work at your public prayers.

Some people think this advice distinctly corrupt. It smells too much of public relations, of concern for public image. After all, whether we are praying in private or in public, we are praying to God: Surely he is the one we should be thinking about; no-one else.

This objection misses the point. Certainly if we must choose between trying to please God in prayer and trying to please our fellow creatures, we must unhesitatingly opt for the former. But that is not the issue. It is not a question of pleasing our human hearers, but of instructing them and edifying them.

The ultimate sanction for this approach is none less than Jesus himself. At the tomb of Lazarus, after the stone has been removed, Jesus looks to heaven and prays, "Father, I thank you that you have heard me. I knew that you always hear me, but I said this on account of the people standing around, that they may believe that you sent me" (John 11:41-42). Here, then, is a prayer of Jesus himself that is shaped in part by his awareness of what his human hearers need to hear.

The point is that although public prayer is addressed to God, it is addressed to God while others are overhearing it. Of course, if the one who is praying is more concerned to impress these human hearers than to pray to God, then rank hypocrisy takes over. That is why Jesus so roundly condemns much of the public praying of his day and insists on the primacy of private prayer (Matt 6:5-8). But that does not mean there is no place at all for public prayer. Rather, it means that public prayer ought to be the overflow of one's private praying. And then, judging by the example of Jesus at the tomb of Lazarus, there is ample reason to reflect on just what my prayer, rightly directed to God, is saying to the people who hear me.

Many facets of Christian discipleship, not least prayer, are rather more effectively passed on by modelling than by formal teaching. Good praying is more easily caught than taught. If it is right to say that we should choose models from whom we can learn, then the obverse truth is that we ourselves become responsible to become models for others. So whether you are leading a service or family prayers, whether you are praying in a small group Bible study or at a convention, work at your public prayers.

8. Pray until you pray

That is Puritan advice. It does not simply mean that persistence should mark much of our praying—though admittedly that is a point the Scriptures repeatedly make. Even though he was praying in line with God's promises, Elijah prayed for rain seven times before the first cloud appeared in the heavens. The Lord Jesus could tell parables urging persistence in prayer (Luke 11:5-13). If some generations need to learn that God is not particularly impressed by long-winded prayers, and is not more disposed to help us just because we are garrulous, our generation needs to learn that God is not impressed by the kind of brevity that is nothing other than culpable negligence. He is not more disposed to help us because our insincerity and spiritual flightiness conspire to keep our prayers brief. Our generation certainly needs to learn something more about persistence in prayer. Even so, that is not quite what the Puritans meant when they exhorted one another to "pray until you pray".

What they meant is that Christians should pray long enough and honestly enough, at a single session, to get past the feeling of formalism and unreality that attends not a little praying. We are especially prone to such feelings when we pray for only a few minutes, rushing to be done with a mere duty. To enter the spirit of prayer, we must stick to it for a while. If we "pray until we pray", eventually we come to delight in God's presence, to rest in his love, to cherish his will. Even in dark or agonized praying, we somehow know we are doing business with God.

If God is the one "who works in you, both to will and to work for his good pleasure" (Phil 2:13), then of course he is the God who by his Spirit helps us in our praying. Every Christian who has learned the rudiments of praying knows by experience at least a little of what this means. The Puritans knew a great deal of it. That is why they exhorted one another to "pray until you pray". Such advice is not to become an excuse for a new legalism: there are startling examples of very short, rapid prayers in the Bible (e.g. Neh 2:4). But in the western world we urgently need this advice, for many of us in our praying are like nasty little boys who ring front door bells and run away before anyone answers.

Pray until you pray.

THESE, THEN, ARE SOME OF THE lessons I have learned from other Christians. But I would not for a moment want to leave the impression that they constitute a rule, a litmus test, still less a 'how-to' manual. The words of Packer in this regard are worth pondering: I start with the truism that each Christian's prayer life, like every good marriage, has in it common factors about which one can generalize and also uniquenesses that no other Christian's prayer life will quite match. You are you, and I am I, and we must each find our own way with God, and there is no recipe for prayer that can work for us like a handyman's do-it-yourself manual or a cookery book, where the claim is that if you follow the instructions you can't go wrong. Praying is not like carpentry or cookery; it is the active exercise of a personal relationship, a kind of friendship, with the living God and his Son Jesus Christ, and the way it goes is more under divine control than under ours. Books on praying, like marriage manuals, are not to be treated with slavish superstition, as if perfection of technique is the answer to all difficulties; their purpose, rather, is to suggest things to try… The only rules are, stay within biblical guidelines and within those guidelines, as John Chapman puts it, "pray as you can and don't try to pray as you can't".[4]

Questions for review and reflection

1. List the positive and negative things you have learned about praying by listening to others pray.

2. List practical ways in which you will commit yourself to improve your prayer life during the next six months.

3. What do Christian preachers and teachers mean when they encourage us to "meditate prayerfully on the word of God"?

Endnotes

1. From DA Carson, *A Call to Spiritual Reformation: Priorities from Paul and His Prayers*, Baker, Grand Rapids, 1992. Abridged with permission of the author.
2. See David H Adeney, 'Personal Experience of God', in *Teach Us To Pray: Prayer in the Bible and the World*, ed. DA Carson, Baker, Grand Rapids, 1990, pp. 309-15.
3. Patrick Johnstone, *Operation World: A day-to-day guide to praying for the world*, 4th edn, STL, Bromley, 1986.
4. Quoted in David Hanes (ed.), *My Path of Prayer*, Worthing, West Sussex, 1981, p. 57.

Feedback on this resource

We really appreciate getting feedback about our resources—not just suggestions for how to improve them, but also positive feedback and ways they can be used. We especially love to hear that the resources may have helped someone in their Christian growth.

You can send feedback to us via the 'Feedback' menu in our online store, or write to us at info@matthiasmedia.com.au.

»TIPS FOR GROUP LEADERS

Studying prayer

PRAYER IS ONE OF THOSE THINGS that reveals a lot about us. If we pray very little, either through laziness or manic over-activity, it says a lot about what we think is important in our Christian lives. Also, our view of prayer—what we think it is and how we should do it—speaks volumes about our whole view of the Christian life (that is, our theology).

It is very important, then, as we come to look at prayer in these Bible studies that we are ready to be challenged in these two areas:

- our own lives, as we take a hard look at our priorities
- our thinking about the Christian life, and how prayer fits in.

The studies in *Bold I Approach* are designed to achieve both of these things. They aim to get Christians thinking about the place prayer has (or doesn't have!) in their lives. And they approach the subject by going back to first principles to think about who God is, how we relate to him, and then how prayer fits into this.

This second emphasis is in some contrast to many books on prayer, which tend to focus more on techniques or programs for improving your prayer life, or else on motivational material that makes you feel guilty enough to get praying again. This is really not the way to approach 'prayer', or any other aspect of Christian living. Instead, we need to go back to the Bible and see what it says, not just about prayer in isolation, but how prayer is part of our whole walk with God.

Study 1 starts by considering the character of God and how we can have a relationship with him. Study 2 moves on to consider how prayer fits into this, the main point being that once you have understood the basic nature of the Christian life, you have pretty much understood prayer.

Studies 3-6 then move onto the specifics of the 'uses' or functions of prayer in our lives, how God wants us to pray, and the problems we encounter.

The appendix by Don Carson can be used in a couple of ways. You can simply leave group members to read and consider it at their leisure. Or you might decide to all read it after the sixth study and discuss it the following week. It contains a number of very helpful practical tips.

Like all our studies, *Bold I Approach* is designed to work in a group on the assumption that the group members have worked through the material in advance. If this is not happening in your group, it will obviously change the way you lead the studies.

If the group is preparing...

If all is well, and the group is well-prepared, then reading through *all* the text, and answering *all* the questions will be time-consuming and probably quite boring. It is not designed to work this way in a group.

The leader needs to go through the study thoroughly in advance and work out how to lead a group discussion using the text and questions as a basis. You should be able to follow the order of the study through pretty much as it is written. But you will need to work out which things you are going to omit, which you are going to glide over quite quickly, and which you are going to concentrate on and perhaps add supplementary discussion questions to.

Obviously, as with all studies, this process of selection

and augmentation will be based on what your *aims* are for this study for your particular group. You need to work out where you want to get to as a main emphasis or teaching point or application point at the end. The material itself will certainly head you in a particular direction, but there will usually be various emphases you can bring out, and a variety of applications to think about.

The slabs of text need to be treated as a resource for discussion, not something to be simply read out. This will mean highlighting portions to talk about, adding supplementary discussion questions and ideas to provoke discussion where you think that would be helpful for your particular group, and so on.

The same is true for the questions. You need to be selective, according to where you want the whole thing to go. Some questions you will want to do fairly quickly or omit altogether. Others you will want to concentrate on—because they are difficult or because they are crucial or both—and in these cases you may want to add a few questions of your own if you think it would help.

You may also need to add some probing questions of your own if your group is giving too many 'pat' answers, or just reproducing the ideas in the text sections without actually grappling with the biblical text for themselves.

There is room for flexibility. Some groups, for example, read the text and do the main body questions in advance, but save the 'Implications' questions for the group discussion.

If the group isn't preparing...

This obviously makes the whole thing a lot harder (as with any study). Most of the above still applies. But if your group is not doing much preparation, your role is even more crucial and active. You will have to be even more careful in your selection and emphasis and supplementary questions—you will have to convey the basic content, as well as develop it in the direction of personal application. Reading through the *whole* study in the group will still be hard going. In your selection, you will probably need to read more sections of text together (selecting the important bits), and you will not be able to glide over comprehension questions so easily.

If the group is not preparing, it does make it harder—not impossible, but a good reason for encouraging your group to do at least some preparation.

Conclusion

No set of printed studies can guarantee a good group learning experience. No book can take the place of a well-prepared thoughtful leader who knows where he or she wants to take the group, and guides them gently along that path.

Our Bible studies aim to be a resource and handbook for that process. They will do a lot of the work for you. All the same, they need to be *used*, not simply followed.

Tony Payne
Series Editor

 **matthias**media

Matthias Media is an evangelical publishing ministry that seeks to persuade all Christians of the truth of God's purposes in Jesus Christ as revealed in the Bible, and equip them with high-quality resources, so that by the work of the Holy Spirit they will:

- abandon their lives to the honour and service of Christ in daily holiness and decision-making
- pray constantly in Christ's name for the fruitfulness and growth of his gospel
- speak the Bible's life-changing word whenever and however they can—in the home, in the world and in the fellowship of his people.

Our resources range from Bible studies and books through to training courses, audio sermons and children's Sunday School material. To find out more, and to access samples and free downloads, visit our website:

www.matthiasmedia.com

How to buy our resources

1. Direct from us over the internet:
  – in the US: www.matthiasmedia.com
  – in Australia: www.matthiasmedia.com.au

2. Direct from us by phone: please visit our website for current phone contact information.

> Register at our website for our **free** regular email update to receive information about the latest new resources, **exclusive special offers**, and free articles to help you grow in your Christian life and ministry.

3. Through a range of outlets in various parts of the world. Visit **www.matthiasmedia.com/contact** for details about recommended retailers in your part of the world, including www.thegoodbook.co.uk in the United Kingdom.

4. Trade enquiries can be addressed to:
  – in the US and Canada: sales@matthiasmedia.com
  – in Australia and the rest of the world: sales@matthiasmedia.com.au

Other Interactive and Topical Bible Studies from Matthias Media

Our Interactive Bible Studies (IBS) and Topical Bible Studies (TBS) are a valuable resource to help you keep feeding from God's word. The IBS series works through passages and books of the Bible; the TBS series pulls together the Bible's teaching on topics such as money or prayer. As at January 2016, the series contains the following titles:

Beyond Eden
GENESIS 1-11
Authors: Phillip Jensen and Tony Payne, 9 studies

Out of Darkness
EXODUS 1-18
Author: Andrew Reid, 8 studies

The Shadow of Glory
EXODUS 19-40
Author: Andrew Reid, 7 studies

The One and Only
DEUTERONOMY
Author: Bryson Smith, 8 studies

Remember the Rock
JOSHUA
Author: Phil Campbell, 6 studies

The Good, the Bad and the Ugly
JUDGES
Author: Mark Baddeley, 10 studies

Famine and Fortune
RUTH
Authors: Barry Webb and David Höhne, 4 studies

God Will Have His King
1 SAMUEL
Author: Des Smith, 9 studies

Renovator's Dream
NEHEMIAH
Authors: Phil Campbell and Greg Clarke, 7 studies

The Eye of the Storm
JOB
Author: Bryson Smith, 6 studies

The Beginning of Wisdom
PROVERBS VOLUME 1
Author: Joshua Ng, 7 studies

Living the Good Life
PROVERBS VOLUME 2
Author: Joshua Ng, 8 studies

The Search for Meaning
ECCLESIASTES
Author: Tim McMahon, 9 studies

Two Cities
ISAIAH
Authors: Andrew Reid and Karen Morris, 9 studies

Kingdom of Dreams
DANIEL
Authors: Andrew Reid and Karen Morris, 9 studies

Burning Desire
OBADIAH AND MALACHI
Authors: Phillip Jensen and Richard Pulley, 6 studies

Warning Signs
JONAH
Author: Andrew Reid, 6 studies

Living by Faith
HABAKKUK
Author: Ian Carmichael, 5 studies

On That Day
ZECHARIAH
Author: Tim McMahon, 8 studies

Full of Promise
THE BIG PICTURE OF THE O.T.
Authors: Phil Campbell and Bryson Smith, 8 studies

The Good Living Guide
MATTHEW 5:1-12
Authors: Phillip Jensen and Tony Payne, 9 studies

News of the Hour
MARK
Authors: Peter Bolt and Tony Payne, 10 studies

Proclaiming the Risen Lord
LUKE 24-ACTS 2
Author: Peter Bolt, 6 studies

Mission Unstoppable
ACTS
Author: Bryson Smith, 10 studies

The Free Gift of Life
ROMANS 1-5
Author: Gordon Cheng, 8 studies

The Free Gift of Sonship
ROMANS 6-11
Author: Gordon Cheng, 8 studies

The Freedom of Christian Living
ROMANS 12-16
Author: Gordon Cheng, 7 studies

Free for All
GALATIANS
Authors: Phillip Jensen and Kel Richards, 8 studies

Walk this Way
EPHESIANS
Author: Bryson Smith, 8 studies

Partners for Life
PHILIPPIANS
Author: Tim Thorburn, 8 studies

The Complete Christian
COLOSSIANS
Authors: Phillip Jensen and Tony Payne, 8 studies

To the Householder
1 TIMOTHY
Authors: Phillip Jensen and Greg Clarke, 9 studies

Run the Race
2 TIMOTHY
Author: Bryson Smith, 6 studies

The Path to Godliness
TITUS
Authors: Phillip Jensen and Tony Payne, 7 studies

From Shadow to Reality
HEBREWS
Author: Joshua Ng, 10 studies

The Implanted Word
JAMES
Authors: Phillip Jensen and Kirsten Birkett, 8 studies

Homeward Bound
1 PETER
Authors: Phillip Jensen and Tony Payne, 10 studies

All You Need to Know
2 PETER
Author: Bryson Smith, 6 studies

The Vision Statement
REVELATION
Author: Greg Clarke, 9 studies

Bold I Approach
PRAYER
Author: Tony Payne, 6 studies

Cash Values
MONEY
Author: Tony Payne, 5 studies

Sing for Joy
SINGING IN CHURCH
Author: Nathan Lovell, 6 studies

The Blueprint
DOCTRINE
Authors: Phillip Jensen and Tony Payne, 9 studies

Woman of God
THE BIBLE ON WOMEN
Author: Terry Blowes, 8 studies